NEW YORK TIMES BESTSELLING AUTHOR

MAX LUCADO

GLORY DAYS

LIVING YOUR PROMISED LAND LIFE NOW

WRITTEN BY KEVIN AND SHERRY HARNEY

THOMAS NELSON
Since 1798

NASHVILLE   MEXICO CITY   RIO DE JANEIRO

Glory Days Study Guide

Copyright © 2015 by Max Lucado

Published in Nashville, Tennessee, by Thomas Nelson. Thomas Nelson is a registered trademark of Thomas Nelson, Inc.

Published in association with Anvil II Management, Inc.

Thomas Nelson, Inc. titles may be purchased in bulk for educational, business, fundraising, or sales promotional use. For information, please e-mail SpecialMarkets@ ThomasNelson.com.

All Scripture quotations, unless otherwise indicated, are taken from The Holy Bible, *New International Version®*, *NIV®*. Copyright © 1973, 1978, 1984, 2011 by Biblica, Inc.™ Used by permission. All rights reserved worldwide.

Scripture quotations marked NKJV are taken from the New King James Version. Copyright © 1982 by Thomas Nelson, Inc. Used by permission. All rights reserved.

Scripture quotations marked NLT are taken from the Holy Bible, *New Living Translation*, copyright © 1996, 2004. Used by permission of Tyndale House Publishers, Inc., Wheaton, Illinois. All rights reserved.

Any Internet addresses (websites, blogs, etc.) and telephone numbers in this book are offered as a resource. They are not intended in any way to be or imply an endorsement by Thomas Nelson, nor does Thomas Nelson vouch for the content of these sites and numbers for the life of this book.

Cover design: Micah Kandros
Interior design: Matthew Van Zomeren

ISBN: 978-0-7180-3597-6

First Printing July 2015 / Printed in the United States of America

CONTENTS

OF NOTE

The quotations interspersed throughout this study guide and the introductory comments are excerpts from the book *Glory Days* and the video curriculum of the same name by Max Lucado. All other resources — including the small group questions, session introductions, and between-sessions materials — have been written by Kevin and Sherry Harney.

A WORD FROM MAX LUCADO

Have you ever felt beat up, outcast, disheartened, or dejected? If you have, you are in good company. The Israelites, God's chosen people, felt like this for forty long years as they wandered in the desert. But then, after four decades of discouragement, hope was on the horizon. God raised up a new leader named Joshua. The people's time in the wilderness furnace was coming to an end. The land of milk and honey was beckoning. The Glory Days were there for the taking.

They still are for us today. In these six sessions, we will discuss how God brings us out of the difficulties of our past. How we must let go of our "can't do" attitude if we want to claim our Promised Land. How we can bring down strongholds and enter into our Glory Days. We will also discuss how God wants us to pray boldly, how we must always choose to believe that he fulfills his promises, and how he promises to not only be with us through the trials of this life but also fight on our behalf.

Expect to be challenged. After all, the enemy won't go down without a fight. But expect great progress. Life is different on the west side of the Jordan. Breakthroughs outnumber breakdowns. God's promises outweigh personal problems. Victory becomes—dare we imagine—a way of life.

Isn't it time for you to change your mailing address from wilderness wandering to Promised Land living? Your Glory Days await you. I invite you to let these words, this holy declaration, settle deep into your heart as you walk forward into God's will for your life:

These days are Glory Days.
My past is past,
my future is bright,
God's promises are true and his Word is sure.
With God as my helper,
I will be all he wants me to be,
do all he wants me to do,
and receive all he wants me to receive.
These are the Glory Days.

I invite you to walk with me from the desert into the Promised Land filled with the presence, power, and glory of the Living God.

THESE DAYS ARE GLORY DAYS

The Promised Land—hope, life, passionate faith, fertile relationships. Should these be the exception or the rule? The book of Joshua helps us see the wilderness is not our true home and the Promised Land awaits all those who are ready to enter. Glory Days are just around the corner, just across the river, close enough to touch. So prepare yourself and step forward. Your Glory Days await you.

Introduction

Do we ask too much of God? Do we desire more than we should? Is God weary of our longings and dreams? In *The Weight of Glory*, C. S. Lewis responds to these questions this way:

> It would seem that our Lord finds our desires not too strong, but too weak. We are half-hearted creatures, fooling about with drink and sex and ambition when infinite joy is offered us, like an ignorant child who wants to go on making mud pies in a slum because he cannot imagine what is meant by the offer of a holiday at the sea. We are far too easily pleased.[1]

As the people of Israel wandered in the wilderness, they looked back on their time in Egypt with selective memory. Although they had been in slavery, beaten, and oppressed ... at least they'd had basic food. After God delivered them from Egypt with a powerful hand, parted the Red Sea, and rained heavenly bread from the sky, they looked over their shoulder and cried, "We remember the fish we ate in Egypt at no cost—also the cucumbers, melons, leeks, onions and garlic" (Numbers 11:5).

The Israelites stood in the wilderness with the Promised Land ahead of them and Egypt behind them. But instead of dreaming of the Glory Days that awaited in a land flowing with milk and honey, they remembered the cucumbers and onions of Egypt.

It is time to march, run, skip, and press forward. No matter how good things might seem in the rearview mirror, what lies ahead can be better. It is time to dream big, to ask of God with boldness, and to believe that our Glory Days are ahead of us.

We must always choose to believe God fulfills his promises.

Talk About It

Welcome to the first session of Glory Days: Living Your Promised Land Life Now. *If you or any of your fellow group members do not know one another, take some time to introduce yourselves. Then, to get things started, discuss one of the following questions:*

C. S. Lewis says we can become like children who are content making mud pies in a slum when God offers a holiday by the sea. What are some of the small things we can become entangled in and enamored with that keep us from experiencing the fullness God wants to offer?

or

What are some of the good, big, and beautiful things we can receive from God if we open ourselves to the greatness of his love and the wonder of his generosity?

Our Promised Land is not real estate but a real state of the heart and mind.

Video Teaching Notes

As you watch the video teaching segment for session one, use the following outline to record anything that stands out to you.

The Great American Immigration period: millions of people boarded boats bound for the hopeful shores of America, a land that spoke of a new hope and new beginning

The journey of the Israelites: the highlights and the lowlights

The seven years of conquest represented a fresh start and a new season for the Israelites ... and we need a fresh start and a new season as well.

The book of Joshua dares us to believe the best days of our lives are ahead of us — that God has a Promised Land for us to take.

The Promised Land was the third stop on the Hebrew people's iconic itinerary: first there was Egypt, then the wilderness, and finally Canaan.

Each stop represented a state of mind: the Israelites were enslaved to Pharaoh in Egypt, slaves to fear in the wilderness, and finally people of promise in Canaan.

Canaan symbolizes the Promised Land life we can have right now—a dream of Promised Land living and our Glory Days.

So many of us are living humdrum lives—as if we, like the Israelites, are stuck in the wilderness—but how would the world change if we marched into our Promised Land?

Video Discussion and Bible Study

Take a few minutes with your group members to discuss what you just watched and explore these concepts in Scripture.

1. Think of a time when God led you to a new beginning and a fresh start. What would you have missed if you had refused to follow God into this new chapter of life?

> We must let go of our "can't do" attitude if we want to claim our Promised Land.

2. During this session's teaching, we saw how the people of God had been through hard times of loss, hurt, and brokenness. Their history was peppered with pain, and their memories often brought tears and shame. Why is it important for us to honestly remember the low points, rebellion, and struggles of God's people?

   If we are going to follow God into the Promised Land and experience our Glory Days, why is it essential for us to look back and remember our *own* pain, loss, and struggles?

Pause *at this point and spend three or four minutes in silence as a*
group reflecting on your own life, struggles, rebellion, pain, and loss.
Ask God to help you remember where you have come from so you can
take delight in what he has prepared for your future.

3. **Read Joshua 21:43 – 45.** This glorious and hope-filled sum-
   mary comes near the end of Joshua. It is a highlight of the
   whole history of God's people. What kind of picture do
   these verses paint? What could your life look like if these
   words described the next season of your life?

> God promises to not only be with us
> through the trials of this life but also fight
> on our behalf.

4. Israel's pilgrimage to freedom began in Egypt, continued
   in the wilderness, and culminated in the Promised Land.
   Talk as a group about each of these chapters in the journey
   of God's people:

Egypt

   • What did God's people experience?

   • What challenges did they face?

- How was God present and at work?

- What lessons did they learn?

The Wilderness

- What did God's people experience?

- What challenges did they face?

- How was God present and at work?

- What lessons did they learn?

Canaan (The Promised Land)

- What did God's people experience?

- What challenges did they face?

- How was God present and at work?

- What lessons did they learn?

5. **Read Romans 8:37–39, Philippians 4:4–7,** and **Colossians 3:15–17.** The Promised Land is not a physical place but a spiritual space. It is the space in which we live when we understand who Jesus is and who we can become as we follow him. What do these passages tell us about ourselves and how we should live as we walk with Jesus?

What is one way you can walk more closely with Jesus in the coming weeks so you can experience the promises declared in these passages?

6. **Read Exodus 15:22–24, 16:1–3,** and **17:1–4.** What patterns do you see in the attitudes and words of God's people? How do we tend to act just like the people of Israel when it comes to facing challenging and difficult life circumstances?

What are some of the dangerous consequences of a complaining and negative spirit?

7. As discussed in the video, *we can be out of Egypt, but Egypt's not out of us!* Even when we know Jesus and are set free from our sins, we can still live in bondage. What are some of the ways Christians continue to live as if they are in Egypt (the land of bondage and oppression) even after coming to faith in the Savior?

What is one way you see yourself going back to attitudes and actions from your old life? How can your group members pray for you and support you as you seek to walk out of the past and into the Promised Land of God's goodness, grace, and freedom?

> God invites us to enter Canaan, but there is one condition. We must turn our backs on the wilderness.

8. **Read 2 Corinthians 3:16 – 18.** This passage notes a number of things that happen when we follow Jesus and walk with him into the Glory Days he has prepared for us. Describe what each of these can look like in our lives each day:

   • We see God with unveiled faces ...

   • We live in the freedom of the Spirit ...

   • We are transferred into Jesus' image ...

9. What is keeping you from walking out of the desert and into the Promised Land? What will you begin doing, or stop doing, in the coming week so you can move toward God's plan for your life?

> God's promises outweigh personal problems.

Closing Prayer

Take time as a group to pray in any of the following directions:

- Thank God for the good and wonderful blessings he gives with such freedom and love.
- Pray for clarity as you look in the rearview mirror of life and ask God to protect you from idealizing the past.
- Ask God to show you what wilderness attitudes and behaviors you need to leave behind as you enter into the Promised Land he has prepared for you.
- Pray for diligence and discipline in reading God's Word on a daily basis so you can have ever-present encouragement to move forward in your faith.
- Ask God to make you discontent with simply believing in Jesus and pray you will become more like Jesus in every way.

> Our Promised Land isn't a physical territory; it is a spiritual reality.

BETWEEN SESSIONS

Reflect further on the content covered during this session by exploring additional material from Scripture and from the book Glory Days.

Personal Reflection

Take time in personal reflection to think about the following questions:

- As I look back on my life, when have I experienced Glory Days and a deep sense of God's presence and leading? What was I doing and how was I living during this season that propelled me into God's Promised Land living?
- What attitudes and actions am I holding on to that are keeping me in the wilderness and out of the Promised Land? What do I need to do to let go of these?
- What can I begin doing today to embrace the Glory Days God wants to give me and take steps into God's Promised Land?

With God's help you can close the gap between the person you are and the person you want to be … indeed, the person God made you to be.

Personal Actions

Now take some time to put the principles discussed during this session into practice.

Glory Days Declaration

Declare the words below as you begin each morning during the coming week. Think about the words. Make this a confident prayer. Thank God these things are true. Ask the Holy Spirit to help you walk boldly forward into the Promised Land life that is prepared for you.

> *These days are Glory Days.*
> *My past is past,*
> *my future is bright,*
> *God's promises are true and his Word is sure.*
> *With God as my helper,*
> *I will be all he wants me to be,*
> *do all he wants me to do,*
> *and receive all he wants me to receive.*
> *These are the Glory Days.*

Three Chapters in Your Life

During this session, we looked at three stages in the Israelites' history. The first was about bondage, the second was about wandering, and the third was a time of Glory Days. Reflect on these three stages in your life. What does each one look like?

Egypt: a time of bondage, slavery, and oppression

- What was your life like before you knew Jesus and experienced his forgiveness and deliverance?

- How did God set you free? How has your life changed since putting your trust in Jesus?

- Why is it important to never idealize this past chapter of your life?

The Wilderness: a time of wandering, wondering if God is strong enough, and wasting time walking in circles

- What do you need to protect against so you do not wander back into the wilderness?

- How can you guard against wilderness attitudes and actions that can cause you to walk in spiritual circles?

- When do you tend to doubt God's powerful presence in your life and his plan for your future? How can you battle against those attitudes?

Canaan (the Promised Land): Glory Days of abundance, fruitfulness, forward movement, victory, and spiritual maturity

- What are some of the Promised Land experiences in which you are engaged right now? How can you grow in these areas of your life?

- How can you keep your heart and eyes fixed on Glory Days living and avoid letting your mind wander back to Egypt or the wilderness?

- How will you thank God and celebrate the good gifts of the Promised Land? What will you do to move deeper and deeper into the Glory Days lifestyle that God longs for you to experience?

Expect to be challenged. After all, the enemy won't go down without a fight. But expect great progress.

Glory Days Dreaming

The Glory Days that God has for his children are bigger, more beautiful, and more abundant than you can imagine. Spend some time to prayerfully dream about what God might want for you in some of the areas listed below. Note this is not about your desires, your "bucket list," or your self-centered pursuits; it is about God's will and the Promised Land he has for you.

What is God's dream and will for your relationship with him?

What is God's dream and will for your engagement in the local church?

What is God's dream and will for how you love and serve the hurting?

What is God's dream and will for your close relationships (family and friends)?

What is God's dream and will for how you spend your free time?

What is God's dream and will for how you use the resources he has placed in your care?

Isn't it time for you to change your mailing address from the wilderness to the Promised Land? Your Glory Days await you.

Recommended Reading

As you reflect on what God is teaching you through this session, read chapter 1 of *Glory Days* by Max Lucado. In preparation for your next session, read chapters 2 – 4.

Journal, Reflections, and Notes

INHERIT YOUR INHERITANCE

The God of heaven and earth offers grace, power, hope, abundant life, joy beyond measure, purpose, and every spiritual blessing that heaven holds. Our part? Receive it. We must open our hearts and lives to embrace the heavenly inheritance he purchased with his own life. What could possibly keep God's children from freely receiving what God freely gives? That, indeed, is the question!

Introduction

He had every reason to say, "I can't!" He had been a killer of Christians. He had persecuted the people of God, ravaged churches, and brutalized the people who were now his spiritual family. When God called Saul to serve him and changed his name to "Paul," the former persecutor of the church could have built a case as to why God could not bless or use someone like him.

She was a foreigner—a stranger in a strange land. She was a widow with no rights or privilege in the ancient world. "I can't" could have been her life motto. Had Ruth known at the time that God would prepare a path for her to become part of the lineage of the promised Messiah, she would have been as shocked as anyone.

He had fallen, and fallen hard. Although David was called "a man after God's heart," he had followed his lust down a road of covetousness, adultery, and murder. In his brokenness and in the aftermath of his rebellion, he could have lived out the rest of his days hiding behind the epitaph, "I can't."

The Bible is a laundry list of unlikely people who God used in spite of their weaknesses, sins, folly, and flat-out disobedience. When undeserving rebels come home and receive their heavenly inheritance, everything changes. When we inherit the inheritance God offers:

Prisoners of war become queens ... just ask Esther.

Fear-filled and denying fishermen turn into Spirit-filled evangelists ... just ask Peter.

Barren women become the mothers of nations ... just ask Sarah.

Trembling farmers turn into mighty warriors ... just ask Gideon.

What's your story? If you have received the inheritance God offers through Jesus, it is time to leave the wastelands of "I can't" and walk into the Promised Land of "look what God can do!"

God's power alters the score.

Talk About It

To get things started for this second session, discuss one of the following questions:

If you are living in the Promised Land of God's amazing inheritance, what have you received, and how is this reality changing your life?

or

If you have not yet left the wilderness to embrace your life in the Promised Land, what is standing in the way?

Conversion is more than a removal of sin. It is a deposit of power.

Video Teaching Notes

As you watch the video teaching segment for session two, use the following outline to record anything that stands out to you.

Frances Cabrini's story of courage and hope in becoming the voice, guardian, and mother to the American immigrants

Why we need to declare war on "I can't" living

Joshua had reason to say "I can't" and make excuses for why he couldn't lead the people:

Excuse #1: Moses was dead

Excuse #2: The people were not ready

Excuse #3: The Canaanites were too powerful

The Hebrews had the land of Canaan because their loving Father declared it.

The book of Joshua is not about earning a reward but receiving an inheritance.

The best-kept secret in Christendom is that we already have everything we need to be everything God desires.

What happens when we don't know about our inheritance

What happens when we don't believe in our inheritance

What God could do if his people embraced his powerful inheritance

The Promised Land life is yours for the taking. Make the mental shift from the wilderness to Canaan.

Video Discussion and Bible Study

Take a few minutes with your group members to discuss what you just watched and explore these concepts in Scripture.

1. When you first understood that God wanted to offer you an inheritance beyond what you could imagine, what obstacles got in the way of you fully receiving it?

2. In the video, we saw that when Frances Cabrini came to America, many people told her she could not impact the world around her, and yet she pressed on. What are some of the "you can't" declarations you have faced? How have you pressed through them?

> Don't measure your life by your ability; measure it by God's.

3. **Read Joshua 1:1–6.** Joshua and the people were facing some very real and legitimate obstacles, which could have caused fear to creep into their hearts and kept them in the wilderness instead of entering the land of God's promise. Discuss briefly how the following could have stopped their forward progression:

   • Moses' death (the passion of a longtime leader whom they trusted)

- The mass of people who needed to be moved, fed, and provided for

- The nations in front of them with reputations as fierce warriors

- Fear of an uncertain future in a land they did not know

How did God seek to strengthen Joshua and give him confident hope to press forward?

4. Think about a time you faced deep loss, fear, or a sense that the road ahead of you was too hard to travel in your own strength. How did God draw near you, fortify you with power, and help you move into his inheritance?

5. As you look at your future and where you believe God is leading you, what obstacles might you face? How can the members of your group come alongside to encourage you to press forward into God's inheritance for your life?

6. **Read Joshua 1:7 – 9.** What did God say to Joshua to empower him to press boldly outward from the wilderness into the land of inheritance? How can these words also uplift and inspire you to move forward into God's inheritance?

> Victory is certain because the victory is God's.

7. God wanted Joshua to keep the Lord's teachings and holy commands continually in his mind and on his lips. Why is it essential for us to immerse ourselves in the truth and teaching of the Bible if we are going to press into God's inheritance?

What disciplines should followers of Jesus have in their lives when it comes to reading, studying, and following the instruction given in the Bible?

8. In the video, Max told a story about receiving the gift of a car from his father. Tell about a time you received a gift that was clearly undeserved. What did experiences like that teach you about God's grace and the gift of the inheritance he wants to freely give you?

9. **Read Joshua 1:3–4, 24:28,** and **Ephesians 1:3.** Why is it so important for us to understand that our inheritance from God is a *gift* and not something we have *earned*?

10. **Read John 1:12–13, Romans 8:14–17, 2 Corinthians 5:16–18,** and **Hebrews 13:20–21.** According to these passages (and others you know), what does God promise to give as a spiritual inheritance to his children? What are ways you are already experiencing and enjoying some of these blessings?

How can the members of your group pray for you and encourage you to press into entering God's inheritance for your life?

Christ's portion is our portion! Whatever he has, we have!

Closing Prayer

Take time as a group to pray in any of the following directions:

- Thank God for the amazing inheritance he has given to his children. Be specific and passionate in your thankfulness ... God has been good!
- Ask for courage as you see obstacles and roadblocks in your path. Pray for power to press on and overcome.
- Confess your "I can'ts." Ask God for confidence to become an "I can" Christian as you work in partnership with God's Holy Spirit in you.
- If you thought of a good gift God has given you during this session, thank him for his inexpressible generosity.
- Pray for fellow group members to walk out of the wilderness and into the Promised Land that God has waiting for them.

The Promised Land property has been placed in your name.

BETWEEN SESSIONS

Reflect further on the content covered during this session by exploring additional material from Scripture and from the book Glory Days.

Personal Reflection

Take time in personal reflection to think about the following questions:

- What is my deepest "I can't" attitude that I have *not yet faced*? What do I need to do to address this area of fear and resistance?
- What gracious gifts and spiritual blessings has God given to me that I have never really thanked him for (in a proper and passionate way)? How can I express my gratitude?
- What fears has God brought me through in the past? How can God's faithfulness in the past prepare me for greater victories in the future?
- How can I help others discover the great inheritance God wants to give them?

> We have to choose — just like Joshua did — to put our "I can'ts" behind us and realize God can.

Personal Actions

Now take some time to put the principles discussed during this session into practice.

Naming Your "I Can'ts"

Make a list of three to five "I can'ts" you have faced *in your past* and pressed through with the help and power of God.

"I Can't" #1: _____

How did God help you press through, break free, and walk in his power and victory?

"I Can't" #2: _____

How did God help you press through, break free, and walk in his power and victory?

"I Can't" #3: _____

How did God help you press through, break free, and walk in his power and victory?

"I Can't" #4: _____

How did God help you press through, break free, and walk in his power and victory?

"I Can't" #5: _____

How did God help you press through, break free, and walk in his power and victory?

Now make a list of two or three "I can'ts" you are facing _right now_:

"I Can't" #1: _____

How does God want you to press through, break free, and walk in his power and victory in this area?

"I Can't" #2: _____

How does God want you to press through, break free, and walk in his power and victory in this area?

"I Can't" #3: _____

How does God want you to press through, break free, and walk in his power and victory in this area?

Wilderness people say, "These are difficult days. I'll never get through them." Promised Land people say, "These days are Glory Days. God will get me through."

Doing What You Can't Do

God wants to do things in you and through you that you simply can't do on your own. But God wants to have you partner with him in these things. He gives the strength, but you have to accept it and walk in his resurrection power. Choose one or two items from the list that follows and write down what you know God wants you to do in his power. List the action, attitudes, and steps you need to take. Then pray for his power and start walking!

❑ Extending forgiveness to someone who has wronged you
❑ Breaking a bad habit
❑ Overcoming an addiction
❑ Controlling your tongue
❑ Taming your temper
❑ Dealing with inappropriate sexual desires
❑ Developing a specific spiritual discipline
❑ Learning to give and be generous
❑ Some other area of growth: _____

Area #1:

Area that needs to change: _____

Specific changes you know God wants to see happen in you:

Your prayer for strength, transformation, and discipline to walk in God's ways:

Area #2:

Area that needs to change: _____

Specific changes you know God wants to see happen in you:

Your prayer for strength, transformation, and discipline to walk in God's ways:

Faith in Action

Frances Cabrini put her faith into action. She counted the cost. She made waves. She built things. When Frances left this life and saw her Savior face to face, she left behind a legacy. Schools, hospitals, orphanages, and changed lives existed where there had been sickness, loneliness, abandonment, and confusion.

What could your group members do, in community, to impact a life, a neighborhood, a school, a community, or a ministry? What could you do that would have lasting impact on others and reveal the Promised Land that is breaking into your world through people who have inherited their inheritance? Write down a few ideas and talk about these as a group the next time you meet.

Ideas for world-impacting group actions:

1.

2.

3.

Leave every "I can't" behind you. Set your "God can" ahead of you. Get ready to cross the Jordan.

Recommended Reading

As you reflect on what God is teaching you through this session, read chapters 2–4 of *Glory Days* by Max Lucado. In preparation for your next session, read chapters 5–8.

Journal, Reflections, and Notes

_____

_____

_____

_____

_____

_____

_____

_____

_____

_____

_____

_____

_____

_____

_____

_____

_____

_____

_____

_____

_____

_____

_____

_____

_____

WALK CIRCLES AROUND JERICHO

Impossible situations, impenetrable walls, and overwhelming odds ... every one of us will face them. The question is not, "Will I deal with situations that are beyond my abilities and strength?" The question is, "Will I try to deal with these challenges alone?" The answer to this question makes all the difference in the world.

Introduction

The walls of Jericho still stand, looming, brooding over our lives, but they are no longer made of stones and mortar. Those walls fell down long ago when Joshua and the people of God marched in circles around them, blew trumpets, and shouted! The walls God's people today face look different, but they nevertheless stand in the way of victory, blocking us from entering fully into the joy of God's plans for our lives.

Consider Renaldo. He loves Jesus and has confessed his sins and need for a Savior. He is seeking to walk in God's ways, but he still faces the walls of Jericho—a hidden addiction to pornography. Over and over again he makes a commitment to stop but continues to click the mouse to enter the familiar and profane world of images and lust. He has quit a hundred times in the past year—and he wants this behavior purged from his life—but as hard as he works in his own power to break down the wall ... there it stands. Why can't he find victory?

Or consider Cindy. She has been a follower of Jesus since she was a girl. She grew up in a good Christian home and is serious about her faith ... it is real! Yet she also faces the walls of Jericho on a weekly basis. For Cindy, the thick walls come in the form of worry. She knows God loves her, believes Jesus is on the throne of her life, and feels the Holy Spirit alive in her heart, but still is often paralyzed by anxiety. She tries to get past it, seeks to ignore it, and even acts as if it is not there. But the Promised Land of peace and trust seem to be on the other side of the wall, and she can't figure out what it will take to knock it down.

These walls in our lives take many shapes and forms: addiction, fear, loneliness, materialism, rage, jealousy, pride, insecurity, prejudice, a grumbling spirit, and more. As Christians, we want to learn how to circle the walls of our Jericho and watch them fall with an earthshaking and future-changing crash.

But the walls remain, keeping us from experiencing Promised Land living.

In many cases, we are doing all we can to break down the walls. We pound at them with our fists. We use all our energy to chip and chisel away at them. Indeed, we find ourselves weary, exhausted, and discouraged from the effort. Then we finally look up, beyond the walls and toward heaven, to the God who is bigger than Jericho's walls.

It is at this point we wonder, *Could it be that though I can't make the walls fall on my own, victory could be close in partnership with God?* When we come to this place, we are ready to fight one more time. And this time, we will follow God's battle plan.

> God has already promised a victory. And he has provided weapons for the fight.

Talk About It

To get things started for this third session, discuss one of the following questions:

If the walls of Jericho represent obstacles that keep you from entering fully into God's Promised Land life, what specific forms do those walls of Jericho take for you?

or

> How have you fought, struggled, and tried to break down these walls in your own power? What has been the result?

> Every battle, ultimately, is a spiritual battle.
> Every conflict is a contest with Satan and
> his forces.

Video Teaching Notes

As you watch the video teaching segment for session three, use the following outline to record anything that stands out to you.

Dr. Martin Luther King Jr. was willing to face obstacles and march on the walls of his Jericho with God leading the way.

What the walls of Jericho represent . . . to the Israelites and to us

How we can understand and own the victory of God

God's battle plan and strategy for victory is different than ours.

We must break down strongholds ... what are ours?

How we attack strongholds, conquer the Promised Land, and walk in victory

The weapons God has given us for the conquest

We are not victims of Jericho — we *can* be steadfast and immovable in the power of the Lord.

A stronghold is a false premise that denies God's promise. It attempts to magnify the problem and minimize God's ability to solve it.

Video Discussion and Bible Study

Take a few minutes with your group members to discuss what you just watched and explore these concepts in Scripture.

1. Dr. Martin Luther King Jr. faced real enemies, threats, deep personal fear, and temptation to quit the fight. Think about Dr. King or another person in history whose willingness to enter a battle side by side with God has served as an example and inspiration for you. What impact has this person's life made on your world?

2. **Read Joshua 1:5–6, 1:10–11, and 6:1–5.** What do these passages say about God's part in winning the victory and bringing down the walls of Jericho? What do you think this means for you? How does God want to be involved in the battles you face?

> The question is not, will you overcome?
> It is, when will you overcome?

3. When was a time you battled, worked hard, and tried to find victory in your own power—but found yourself beating your head against the walls of Jericho with no real victory?

When was a time you looked to God, followed his ways, and became a partner with him in a spiritual battle you faced? How did the walls come down?

> When mighty Jericho crumbled, the untoppleable fortress met the unstoppable force.

4. If you want to see Jericho fall, you have to stop labeling yourself and others. Stop listening to the lies. Stop believing there is no hope for change or a new beginning. What is a negative attitude you need to put aside and stop letting reside in your mind?

5. Instead of negative thinking and attitudes, you need to declare, "The boundary lines have fallen for me in pleasant places; surely I have a delightful inheritance" (Psalm 16:6). What are some other biblical passages and truths you can keep in your mind and heart and on your lips to help you remember the goodness of God and his great promises?

Why is it important to meditate on these good promises and truths?

Live out of your inheritance, not your circumstance.

6. **Read Joshua 6:6–11.** In this passage Joshua gathered his leaders—both the priests and military—and shared God's plan of attack. How do you think the people responded to these unconventional and strange instructions? How do you think the battle would have gone if Joshua and the people had attacked the city with conventional warfare strategies?

7. What instructions does God give his people today that might seem strange in the eyes of our modern culture? Why is it important for us to follow God's instructions, even when they don't make sense to us?

8. **Read Ephesians 6:10–13** and **2 Corinthians 10:3–5.** The Bible is clear that all believers will face spiritual battles. Who is our enemy, and what are some of his tactics? Why must we identify the presence and attack points of the enemy?

> Every level of inheritance requires a disinheritance from the devil. Satan must be moved off before the saint can move in.

9. What counsel would you give Christians who act as if they are defeated and unable to stand against the enemy's tactics? What does the Bible say about God's power to do battle against the works of the evil one?

10. In this session, we looked at some of the weapons God has given us to do battle against the enemy of our souls. Talk about how each of these weapons can empower us to walk in victory:

- Songs, praise, and worship

- Reading, studying, and memorizing Scripture

- Prayer, petition, and thanksgiving

What specific steps can you take to increase the place of worship, Scripture, and prayer in your daily life? And how can your group members encourage you and keep you accountable to grow in each of these areas in the coming weeks?

You are a coheir with Christ. Every attribute of Jesus is at your disposal.

Closing Prayer

Take time as a group to pray in any of the following directions:

- Thank God for the people in your life who have lived (and even died) showing you what it means to live with bold confidence in God's victory and power.
- Pray for power, in Jesus' name, to never seek to fight your spiritual battles in your own strength. Ask for Jesus to help you be a partner in the battle he has already won.
- Ask God to give you courage to follow his battle plans and life instructions, even when they don't fully make sense to you.
- Ask God to help fellow group members in any area in which they are struggling to walk in the victory of Jesus.

Life will always bring challenges. But God will always give strength to face them.

BETWEEN SESSIONS

Reflect further on the content covered during this session by exploring additional material from Scripture and from the book Glory Days.

Personal Reflection

Take time in personal reflection to think about the following questions:

- Who are the people who are looking to me as a spiritual example? Are they seeing a courageous, bold, God-following Joshua? How can I live with greater courage for their sake?
- What is a Jericho wall I have been running into and beating my head against for a long time? Are my battle strategies mine or God's? If I have been fighting in my own strength, what battle plan do I think God would have me follow?
- When was a time that God called me to follow his ways and I felt they were strange ... but I followed anyway. How did God show up? How was he victorious? What keeps me from boldly following God today?

To live in the Promised Land, you must face your Jericho.

Personal Actions

Now take some time to put the principles discussed during this session into practice.

Declare It!

Using your Bible or a Bible concordance, make a list of ten truths from Scripture that remind you of God's goodness, victory, power, and love. You might also call or text a few Christian friends and mentors to ask for a favorite biblical truth and passage that strengthens their hearts.

Truth #1: _____

Passage: _____

_____

Truth #2: _____

Passage: _____

_____

Truth #3: _____

Passage: _____

_____

Truth #4: _____

Passage: _____

_____

Truth #5: _____

Passage: _____

_____

Truth #6: _____

Passage: _____

_____

Truth #7: _____

Passage: _____

_____

Truth #8: _____

Passage: _____

_____

Truth #9: _____

Passage: _____

_____

Truth #10: _____

Passage: _____

_____

Choose two or three of these passages and commit them to memory. Whenever the enemy begins to whisper lies, or your mind begins to wander to negative and ungodly thinking, let these truths wash over your heart and fill your thoughts. Declare the truth!

We must move from false premises to God's promises.

Name It and Fight It

In this session, Max discussed how a stronghold is a false premise that denies God's promise. The following are some common strongholds that Christians face today. As you read this list, ask for the Holy Spirit's discernment and check any that apply (or add others):

- ❑ *God could never forgive me* (stronghold of **guilt**)
- ❑ *I could never forgive that person* (stronghold of **resentment**)
- ❑ *Bad things always happen to me* (stronghold of **self-pity**)
- ❑ *I have to be in charge* (stronghold of **pride**)
- ❑ *I don't deserve to be loved* (stronghold of **rejection**)
- ❑ *I'll never recover from this* (stronghold of **defeat**)
- ❑ *I must be good or God will reject me* (stronghold of **performance**)
- ❑ *I'm only as good as I look* (stronghold of **appearance**)
- ❑ *My value equals my possessions* (stronghold of **materialism**)
- ❑ A stronghold I face is _____
- ❑ A stronghold I face is _____

If you are facing one of these strongholds, admit it. Say it. Name it. But don't stay there. Declare the truth of 2 Corinthians 10:4. In the name of Jesus, through his sacrifice on the cross and the glory of the resurrection, *you have the divine power to demolish strongholds*. So, in the name of Jesus, demolish them! Watch the walls fall down!

Start Marching

Day after day, the people of God marched around the city of Jericho. On the seventh day, God called them to march around the city seven times. They could have quit at this point and said, "That's enough! This is getting ridiculous!" But they marched, blew the trumpets, and shouted ... just as God instructed. You know the rest of the story. The walls came down!

Is there an area of your life where you have marched for six days and then given up? Maybe victory is one more march away. If you have given up on something God has called you to do because you have become weary, consider reengaging in God's plan for you ... and start marching again.

Write down an area where you marched, fought, and tried to follow God but then gave up.

What would it take for you to begin marching again? How can you start today?

Keep marching ... for all you know this may be the day the walls come down.

Recommended Reading

As you reflect on what God is teaching you through this session, read chapters 5–8 of *Glory Days* by Max Lucado. In preparation for your next session, read chapters 9–12.

Journal, Reflections, and Notes

_____

_____

_____

_____

_____

_____

_____

_____

_____

_____

_____

_____

_____

_____

_____

_____

_____

_____

_____

_____

_____

_____

_____

_____

_____

_____

PRAY AUDACIOUS PRAYERS

We talk to God. We cry out to him. That's part of being a Christian ... we pray. But do we pray with bold confidence and shocking audacity? Do we know God hears us and actually responds to our prayers? If we watch Joshua closely and learn from his example, our prayers will be more frequent, more courageous, and more powerful!

Introduction

Children are often taught to repeat simple prayers as a tool to help them make talking to God a part of their normal day. Maybe you have heard some of these prayers, or perhaps you were taught some of them as a young boy or girl. One example is a common mealtime prayer:

God is great, God is good,
And we thank him for our food;
By God's hand we all are fed,
Give us, God, our daily bread. Amen.

Before bed, many little ones repeat these words:

Now I lay me down to sleep,
I pray the Lord my soul to keep;
May God guard me through the night,
And wake me with the morning light. Amen.

This version of the classic bedtime prayer has a kinder and gentler ending. Some of us actually grew up finishing that prayer with the sobering words, *"If I should die before I wake, I pray the Lord my soul to take."*

What many of these children's prayers have in common is a tone that is simple, rhythmic, and tame. The requests tend to circle around safe topics such as blessing our food, giving us a good night of sleep, placing angels around our beds, and blessing those we love. These prayers don't sound risky, bold, or courageous. They are prayers on training wheels ... starter kits for talking with God.

What is both sad and dangerous is when grown-ups continue to parrot these same words in a mindless routine of pre-bedtime and pre-dining tradition. Such prayers lack a genuine connection with God. These children's prayers are ... well, for children. Grown-up followers of God should learn to take off the training wheels and discover that bold, audacious, and shocking prayers thrill the heart of God and open the hand of the Creator.

> Consult God in all things. Call on him for great things.

Talk About It

To get things started for this fourth session, discuss one of the following questions:

Who taught you to pray? How did that person get you started on this wonderful journey of learning to talk with God?

or

How have you seen your prayer life develop and deepen as you have grown in your Christian faith?

> Live with one ear toward heaven. Keep the line open to God.

Video Teaching Notes

As you watch the video teaching segment for session four, use the following outline to record anything that stands out to you.

During a trip across the Atlantic, the preacher John Wesley prayed boldly for God to calm the stormy seas—and fully expected his prayer to be answered.

Martin Luther prayed bold prayers for his sick friend—*commanding* him to live.

Boldness in prayer is an uncomfortable thought for many, but the truth is that God invites us to storm heaven with such prayers.

An example from Joshua's life of how *not* to pray (the Gibeonite deception)

How asking for God's counsel protects us from the deception of the devil

What God grants to us through the exercise of prayer

An example from Joshua's life of how *to* pray (the audacious sun-stopping prayer)

What bold prayers could change in our world and in our lives

> When the authority of Christ is proclaimed, the work of Satan must stop.

Video Discussion and Bible Study

Take a few minutes with your group members to discuss what you just watched and explore these concepts in Scripture.

1. How do you respond to the story of John Wesley's bold prayer and absolute confidence that God would hear him and stop the storm at sea? Does it feel too bold and almost arrogant? Or does this kind of audacious prayer appeal to you? Explain.

How might your prayer life change if you began praying like John Wesley?

2. Martin Luther wrote, "I attacked God with his own weapons, quoting from Scripture all the promises I could remember, that prayers should be granted." He also prayed these words for a friend who was helping him with the challenging work of reforming the church: "I command thee in the name of God to live because I still have need of thee in the work of reforming the church.... The Lord will never let me hear that thou art dead, but will permit thee to survive me. For this I am praying, this is my will, and may my will be done, because I seek only to glorify the name of God." Imagine you were in a circle of church members and someone prayed like this. What would be your initial response to this level of boldness and confidence in prayer?

Why do you think we often shy away from lifting up prayers with this kind of absolute assurance that God will hear us and answer?

3. **Read Hebrews 4:14–16.** What kind of attitude and out-look does this passage say we should bring to God when we pray? Why can we come to God with this kind of certainty?

What keeps you from praying with such confidence and audacious boldness?

4. **Read Joshua 9:3–19.** What happened in this encounter that caused Joshua and the other leaders to fail to pray and seek the Lord's wisdom? What are some of the things that happen in the flow of a day that might cause you to press forward, rely on your own insight, and miss an opportunity to seek the Lord's guidance through prayer?

What life decision or situation are you presently experiencing that your group members could pray with you about and seek the Lord's leading?

> Consult God in everything. Always.
> Immediately. Quickly.

5. When was a time in your life when you did not think to pray, made a decision, and later regretted not asking God's insight and wisdom?

How might things have turned out differently if you had slowed down, prayed, and received guidance from God in this situation?

6. **Read Proverbs 3:5–6** and **Psalm 27:7–14.** The devil is always looking to derail you, pushing you off the path God has for you, so it is essential for you to seek God's wisdom. What do these passages teach about the importance of seeking God's wisdom through prayer? What are some ways you do this during the flow of a regular day?

Think about a time you sought God's wisdom and waited on an answer from him. How did God speak to you? What means did he use? How did you respond to this clear direction from the Lord?

7. **Read Joshua 10:7 – 14.** Joshua prayed for the "impossible" and discovered that with God, all things really are possible. What is a big prayer—a huge prayer, an impossible prayer—that you simply don't dare lift up to God? If you are willing, invite your group members to join you in praying for this, even if you are still fearful of praying for it.

8. In the video, Max told the story of his friend, Greg Pruett, who invited his ministry leaders at Pioneer Bible translators to pray for God's provision. The result was a shocking and amazing outpouring of resources that had no human explanation. Think about a time when you and others dared to lift up a bold prayer. How did God answer your prayers? In light of experiences like this, why don't we pray with greater frequency and confidence?

9. Joshua faced discouragement, deception, defeat, destruction, and death. But he still prayed and saw God do great things. What challenges in your life right now discourage you and keep you from praying as consistently and boldly as you should? How can your group members fortify you in prayer and help you grow in confidence?

> As you face your battles, respond in prayer—honest, continual, and audacious prayer.

10. There is power when we pray in concert with other believers, joining our voices and faith together. What are some big topics and needs you can gather around and pray for together as a group during the coming weeks?

Closing Prayer

Take time as a group to pray in any of the following directions:

- Pray for the "big topics" you discussed as a group in question 10 above.
- Cry out for faith to pray bigger and bolder prayers.
- Ask God to give you wisdom to seek him and never rely on your own insight.
- Invite the Holy Spirit to help you recognize the voice and work of God with growing clarity.
- Commit to God that you will seek to lift up some sun-stopping and audacious prayers.

> Worry less, pray always.

BETWEEN SESSIONS

Reflect further on the content covered during this session by exploring additional material from Scripture and from the book Glory Days.

Personal Reflection

Take time in personal reflection to think about the following questions:

- What are the boldest prayers I have ever dared to pray? What would it look like if I prayed like this more often and with growing confidence?
- In what situations do I tend to look to my own wisdom instead of praying and asking God to lead me? How can I make sure I don't take action before calling out to God and listening for his guidance?
- Is there a situation in my life where I did not ask God for help and direction and now am in a tough place (like Joshua and the people of Gibeon)? How can I surrender this situation to God and make the best of it?

Jesus spilled his blood for you. You can spill your heart before God.

Personal Actions

Now take some time to put the principles discussed during this session into practice.

Get Specific

We need to be specific as we seek wisdom from God in prayer—we need to ask him clear questions so we will receive specific guidance and direction. So today, take time to ask God some of the following bold questions, expect him to answer in ways you can understand, and then follow his leading.

- "Is this opportunity from you, God?"
- "Are you in this venture, Lord?"
- "Should I take this road, Father?"
- "Can I trust this person in a business relationship?"
- "Who is someone in my life who needs to know about your love and truth? What can I do to show that person you are real?"
- "What is an attitude or behavior I need to repent of and turn away from?"
- "How do you want me to be more generous with my encouragement, time, love, and resources?"

Add questions of your own:

-

-

-

Sun Stand Still

Identify two or three big prayers that you have resisted lifting up to God because you felt they were simply too audacious. Commit to pray these prayers consistently and in faith for the coming two weeks. Pray each day, and ask with bold humility that God grant these requests.

Audacious Prayer #1

Audacious Prayer #2

Keep a journal of your prayers and the answers to those prayers.

My Prayers

God's Answers

Stand Strong and Fight the Fight

Like Joshua, you may face discouragement, deception, defeat, destruction, and even death. Following God in this world is a battle, and the fight is on! You can't quit, give up, or give in — you must stand strong! To that end, write down some of the battles you are facing right now, and then identify actions you can take that will honor God and help you stand strong. Once you have done this, pray bold prayers in faith.

Battle #1

What I am facing:

Action I can (and should) take that will honor God:

My bold and audacious prayer as I enter into this battle:

Battle #2

What I am facing:

Action I can (and should) take that will honor God:

My bold and audacious prayer as I enter into this battle:

Battle #3

What I am facing:

Action I can (and should) take that will honor God:

My bold and audacious prayer as I enter into this battle:

> God's word is a "lamp to our feet" (Psalm
> 119:105), not a spotlight into the future.
> God gives enough light to take the next step.

Recommended Reading

As you reflect on what God is teaching you through this session, read chapters 9–12 of *Glory Days* by Max Lucado. In preparation for your next session, read chapters 13–15.

Journal, Reflections, and Notes

_____

_____

_____

_____

_____

_____

_____

_____

_____

_____

_____

_____

_____

_____

_____

_____

_____

_____

_____

_____

_____

_____

_____

_____

_____

NO FALLING WORDS

In a world where promises are broken and trust is an endangered species, it is easy to become cynical. In a time when false advertisement is so commonplace that it is expected, it is no wonder that pessimism is on the rise. In a culture where politicians can bend the truth to the point of breaking and no one is shocked, it is easy to become distrustful. Is there anyone who can be trusted to keep promises, follow through, and always uphold their word? Joshua learned that he could trust God and believe in his promises with rock-solid confidence. It is time for us to learn the same lesson.

Introduction

A major food company placed these words, in large letters, across the front of the box of their popular cereal: "NOW HELPS SUPPORT YOUR CHILD'S IMMUNITY." The company also boasted the cereal provided "25% daily value of antioxidants and nutrients." These statements certainly seemed impressive, and they were appealing enough to sell lots of cereal. The problem was the company had no hard scientific evidence to support these claims. So, the Federal Trade Commission ordered the company to remove the statements from the boxes of cereal.

This company is not alone when it comes to dubious advertising claims. A well-known shoe company sold lots of sneakers (for more than a hundred dollars a pair) by promising consumers that walking in their shoes activated their glutes, quads, hamstrings, and calves in such a way it burned more calories. The dilemma was these "toning sneakers" had no secret technology. They actually led to more injuries—but no extra weight loss.

Another popular social networking site started sending people an email that said, "Old friends are trying to contact you!" All these people needed to do was pay an extra three dollars to upgrade to a gold membership and they could rekindle old friendships and connect with old romantic interests. More than three million people kicked in the requested money, only to discover their "old friends" were *not* actually trying to contact them. The company ended up paying 9.5 million dollars to customers who had been tricked.[2]

These are just a few examples of false advertising that has become so prevalent in modern commerce that many people don't believe anything advertisers say anymore. Unfortunately, this same cynicism can carry over to other areas of life. It is easy for us to become so disenchanted that we have a hard time believing anyone can be trusted or any promise can be kept.

In a life of broken promises, God keeps his.

Talk About It

To get things started for this fifth session, discuss one of the following questions:

Tell about a time you bought a product that simply did not live up to the advertiser's hype. How did you feel when you realized you had been tricked into buying this product?

or

What are some of the current cultural realities and practices that cause people to become distrustful, cynical, and slow to believe any promises?

Nothing deserves your attention more than God's covenants.

Video Teaching Notes

As you watch the video teaching segment for session five, use the following outline to record anything that stands out to you.

Annie Moore chose to believe her Promised Land was real and acted on those beliefs.

A testimony from a father, written on a napkin, about releasing his daughter to God and trusting in the Lord through the pain

Faith is a choice, and Promised Land people choose to take the risk of trusting in God's promises.

How Joshua's story reveals to us that our God is a promise-keeping God

We live in a world where we hear lots of "falling words"—broken promises, empty vows, pledges made only to be forgotten—but we will never hear them from God.

Why it is important for us to *know*, *remember*, and *meditate* on God's promises

In every situation we can either choose to trust in God's promises with faith or react to our circumstances with fear.

What Wes Bishop's testimony reveals about trusting in God's promises to the very end

God keeps his promises. Trust him.

Video Discussion and Bible Study

Take a few minutes with your group members to discuss what you just watched and explore these concepts in Scripture.

1. Think about a person who has lived (and maybe even died) with a deep trust in the promises of God and unrelenting confidence in his trustworthiness. How has this person's life and faith strengthened you and increased your confidence in God's promises?

2. We live in a world of "falling words, broken promises, empty vows, retracted pledges, and ignored assurances." How have you experienced this sad reality in your life, business dealings, or relationships?

> In this world of falling words and broken promises, do yourself a favor: take hold of the promises of God.

3. How does our society's tendency to shift away from promise keeping and trustworthiness negatively impact the way we view God's promises and assurances? How can we keep trusting God even when other people may not always be trustworthy?

4. Use the napkin-sized space below to write a brief personal testimony of a time you experienced loss but held on to the hand of God. How did you experience his trustworthiness through your difficult season of loss?

If you are comfortable doing so, read your napkin testimony (or invite someone else in your group to read it for you). How has your faith and trust in God increased through this time of struggle in your life?

5. How would you respond to this statement: "Promised Land people stand at the crossroads of belief and disbelief and choose to press into the promises of God"?

What is a crossroads you are facing right now? How can your group members pray for you and support you as you seek to believe God's promises?

Faith is a choice.

6. **Read Joshua 21:43–45.** What do you learn from this passage about how God keeps his promises and upholds his word? What specific promises did God give his people that he kept and fulfilled?

7. The writers of the ancient world often used repetition to indicate what they were saying was important. If writers really wanted to emphasize a point, they would say it three times. Reread Joshua 21:43–45 and notice how many times we are told God kept his promises to his people. In a world of broken promises, how does it feel to know that God always keeps his word?

How are our lives as Christians impacted when we live with absolute confidence that God really does keep his promises?

> Search the Scriptures like a miner digging for gold. Once you find a nugget, grasp it. Trust it. Take it to the bank.

8. **Read Genesis 12:6–9.** God promised the land to Abraham and his descendants about six hundred years before Joshua and the people of God received this "inheritance." God kept his promise, but the timing was certainly not what Abraham and his immediate descendants expected. What is a promise you are still waiting to fully realize and experience? (Let your group members know how they can pray for you during this season of waiting and anticipation.)

9. **Read Romans 8:31–39.** What are some of the promises given in this passage?

- _____

- _____

- _____

- _____

- _____

- _____

How can these promises strengthen your faith and help you live in bold peace if you really believe them?

Press into God's promises. When fears or doubts surface, respond with this thought: But God said ...

Closing Prayer

Take time as a group to pray in any of the following directions:

- Thank God for keeping his promises. Praise him for specific promises he has kept in your life.
- Ask for patience in any area of life where you are still waiting for the complete fulfillment of God's promise.
- Pray for fellow group members to live with absolute and bold confidence in the promises of God.
- If you have a specific Bible passage that represents a promise of God you want to hold on to, read it aloud as a prayer.
- Praise God for the people he has placed in your life who live as a powerful example of trusting his promises with confident assurance.

Our God is a promise-keeping God. If God makes a promise, he keeps it.

BETWEEN SESSIONS

Reflect further on the content covered during this session by exploring additional material from Scripture and from the book Glory Days.

Personal Reflection

Take time in personal reflection to think about the following questions:

- Where and when do I find myself lacking confidence in God's promises? How can I grow my faith so I boldly trust God no matter what I face?
- Who are the people who look to me as an example of Christian maturity? Do they see me as an example of trusting God, his Word, and his promises?
- What crossroad of belief am I confronting right now? What can I do to walk the road of confident trust in the promises of God in this area?

We need to place one determined foot in front of the other on the pathway of faith. Seldom with a skip; usually with a limp.

Personal Actions

Now take some time to put the principles discussed during this session into practice.

Knowing God's Promises

If we are going to trust the promises of God, hold on to them, and be empowered by them, we must *know* them. Reflect now on some of these promises:

- To the **bereaved**: "Weeping may stay for the night, but rejoicing comes in the morning" (Psalm 30:5).
- To the **besieged**: "The righteous person may have many troubles, but the LORD delivers him from them all" (Psalm 34:19).
- To the **sick**: "The LORD sustains them on their sickbed and restores them from their bed of illness" (Psalm 41:3).
- To the **lonely**: "When you pass through the waters, I will be with you" (Isaiah 43:2).
- To the **dying**: "Do not let your hearts be troubled. You believe in God; believe also in me. My Father's house has many rooms ... I am going there to prepare a place for you" (John 14:1–2).
- To the **sinner**: "My grace is sufficient for you" (2 Corinthians 12:9).

Use the space below to add three additional promises from God's Word that have lifted your heart and brought you comfort:

Promise #1:

Promise #2:

Promise #3:

> No words written on paper will ever sustain you like the promises of God.

Lock It into Your Heart and Mind

One of the best things you can do to begin building your trust in God's faithfulness is to memorize Bible passages that contain clear promises from the Lord. Following are a few such passages. During the coming weeks, determine to commit one or more of them to memory:

> No, in all these things we are more than conquerors through him who loved us. For I am convinced that neither death nor life, neither angels nor demons, neither the present nor the future, nor any powers, neither height nor depth, nor anything else in all creation, will be able to separate us from the love of God that is in Christ Jesus our Lord (Romans 8:37–39).

> He gives strength to the weary and increases the power of the weak. Even youths grow tired and weary, and young men stumble and fall; but those who hope in the LORD will renew their strength. They will soar on wings like eagles; they will run and not grow weary, they will walk and not be faint (Isaiah 40:29–31).

> "Come to me, all you who are weary and burdened, and I will give you rest. Take my yoke upon you and learn from me, for I am gentle and humble in heart, and you will find rest for your souls. For my yoke is easy and my burden is light" (Matthew 11:28–29).

> If we confess our sins, he is faithful and just and will forgive us our sins and purify us from all unrighteousness (1 John 1:9).

The Power of a Testimony

In this session, you heard about a man who shared his testimony on a napkin while on an airplane. You also heard about Wes Bishop, a man who was faithful to Christ and cried out to him with confident faith as he drew near the end of his time on earth. You have undoubtedly heard other stories of God's goodness and faithfulness to those who trust in him.

Today, pray about sharing the short napkin testimony you wrote during this session. (If you did not have a chance to do so then, go back to question 4 and write your testimony of God's trustworthiness now.) Then actually share this story with someone during the coming week. If the person is a follower of Jesus, pray that your story will encourage him or her to trust God's promises with greater confidence. If the person is not a Christian, pray that your story will reveal the presence of Jesus and draw his or her heart to God.

> In Jesus every person has hope and the possibility of redemption.

Recommended Reading

As you reflect on what God is teaching you through this session, read chapters 13 – 15 of *Glory Days* by Max Lucado. In preparation for your next session, read chapter 16.

Journal, Reflections, and Notes

GOD FIGHTS FOR YOU

I am never alone. I am not a helpless victim. I might be weak in my own strength, but the God who loves me is strong beyond comprehension. When I face challenges, enemies, and attacks in this world, I can confidently know that God is my defender and he is ready to fight on my behalf. When I believe this, peace floods my heart and I walk through life with bold confidence.

Introduction

Picture this single-frame cartoon. A cute, fluffy, little lamb is walking down a path on its hind legs. The lamb is minding its own business, just strolling along. On the other side of the path are a wolf and a lion, also standing on their hind legs. These two carnivorous creatures have their eyes locked on the lamb—and they look hungry. Their teeth are sharp and their intentions are obviously evil.

If these three were the only characters in the cartoon, we would know how the story ends. We would fear for the lamb ... and rightly so. We could title the cartoon "Lunchtime." And we all know what the main course would be!

But there is one more character in this cartoon, and the presence of this figure changes everything. Walking next to the lamb is his Good Shepherd, Jesus. The lamb is holding the hand of his shepherd, and the shepherd has his eyes locked squarely on the wolf and the lion. Over the head of the lamb is a text bubble that says it all. Just these few simple words: "I'm with him!"

This is the story of the Christian life in a one-frame cartoon. This simple image, while humorous, contains deep theological insights:

We do not walk alone.
We are not unprotected.
We are not helpless victims.

When we walk side by side with our Savior, we discover that our God protects us, watches over us, and, when needed ... fights for us.

When we feel threatened and see the glowing eyes of wolves and lions along the path of life, all we need to do is say and believe these words: "I'm with him!"[3]

Not only does God desire that you live the Promised Land life, but he fights for you so you can.

Talk About It

To get things started for this sixth session, discuss one of the following questions:

When was a time you were walking the road of life and you experienced God's protective presence watching over you?

or

How would a difficult situation you have faced been different if you were truly alone and God was not with you, holding your hand and fighting for you?

This is your inheritance: more victory than defeat, more joy than sadness, more hope than despair.

Video Teaching Notes

As you watch the video teaching segment for session six, use the following outline to record anything that stands out to you.

Lee Nailling's story of the Orphan Train and how he longed for the hope that his father would one day find him and be there to protect him

Nadin Khoury's story: any bully will think twice if they know the person they are antagonizing has an NFL All-Pro receiver on speed dial

Joshua faced big enemies . . . and so do we.

God fought for Joshua and the people of Israel . . . and he will fight for us.

Joshua's final message to the people was that "God did it all"—he surrounded them, was present with them, and fought for them.

God's promise to us is that we will chase away a thousand fears; chase away a thousand negative thoughts; chase away a thousand feelings of guilt and despair.

It falls to us to say no to wilderness living and yes to God's Promised Land living.

Jesus fought for us, won the ultimate victory, and deposited his Spirit within us so we would know that he is fighting for us—and we are worth fighting for.

> So we say with confidence, "The Lord is my helper; I will not be afraid. What can mere mortals do to me?" (Hebrews 13:6).

Video Discussion and Bible Study

Take a few minutes with your group members to discuss what you just watched and explore these concepts in Scripture.

1. What are some of the experiences that make people feel defenseless, vulnerable, and fearful as they walk through life on this planet?

   What are fears you have faced or might even be facing today?

2. In what ways have you tried to protect yourself and create a sense of security to feel safe in this dangerous world?

Why do these man-made defenses never bring ultimate and absolute safety?

3. The story of Nadin Khoury is a heartbreaking account of bullying and the apathy of many passersby. How do you see our culture and world becoming more dangerous and unsafe? Why does this reality make the truth that God will protect us and fight for us even more important as we live out our faith and share the good news of Jesus with others?

4. **Read Joshua 1:5–9.** What promises did God give to Joshua? How would these assurances have made Joshua live with greater boldness and confidence?

The big news of the Bible is not that you fight for God but that God fights for you.

5. Some of God's biblical promises come with conditions and directions. *Our* part is living in such a way that God's promises are unleashed with greater power. What specific direction and guidance did God give Joshua in Joshua 1:7–8? Why were these instructions so important?

6. How does following the teaching of the Bible, studying Scripture, meditating on biblical truth, and living in obedience to God's commands help us experience victory?

How might neglecting the teaching of Scripture get in the way of us fully experiencing the victory God offers?

7. **Read Hebrews 13:5–6.** The word for "helper" in this passage comes from two Greek root words that mean "a shout" and "to run." The picture is one of God running to our aid in tough times. God assures us, "I will be there; nothing could keep me away from you!" How does God run to us when we are facing fearful and painful experiences? What does he say to us in those situations?

In times of need, how can we run to God and shout out for his help?

> The One who made you is with you. The Almighty will never leave or forsake you.

8. **Read Joshua 1:3, 11, 13; 3:5; 4:23; and 23:3, 9–10.** What do you see God doing in these passages? What does he promise to do for his people?

   As you read the book of Joshua (and other portions of the Bible), what other examples do you see of God stepping in, protecting, leading, and fighting for his people?

   How do these biblical accounts give you hope, assurance, and bold confidence as you face battles in your life?

9. In your battles right now, how have you witnessed God showing up, bringing strength, and fighting for you?

10. God fights for us, but he also calls us to fight for his will and ways in the world. In most of the battles Joshua and the people engaged in, they still had to pick up their weapons and enter the fray. What is your role in standing strong, entering the fight, and doing your part in your battles?

How can your group members pray for you and support you as you do your part (in tandem with God) to walk in victory?

March like a Promised Land conqueror.

Closing Prayer

Take time as a group to pray in any of the following directions:

- Thank God for being your Good Shepherd and for walking with you through every dangerous valley. Praise him that he never leaves you alone.
- Pray for those in your world who are bullied, hurting, and forgotten, and who need to know the Good Shepherd.
- Lift up someone in your life who is far from Jesus and does not know there is a God who is ready to step in and fight for him or her. Ask God to give you courage to share the hope and joy of what it means to walk with Jesus.
- Ask God to help you be so aware of his presence that you live with a fearless confidence as you walk in the wisdom of the Holy Spirit.

God not only stays with you ... but he also fights for you.

IN THE COMING DAYS

Reflect further on the content covered during this session by exploring additional material from Scripture and from the book Glory Days.

Personal Reflection

Take time in personal reflection to think about the following questions:

- How has God revealed both his power and love through hard times in my life?
- In what area of my life am I still seeking to be strong in my own power and not calling out to God for help? How can I begin to invite God in and let him know I need his deliverance and strength?
- In what ways am I sitting back and expecting God to fight for me, when he is calling me to rise up, take action, and join in the battle? What can I do in the coming weeks to partner with God?
- What person in my life is in the midst of a massive battle? How is God calling me to stand at that person's side and fight for him or her? What actions can I take to be an agent of God's presence and power?

You were not made to quake in fear. You were not made to be beholden to your past. You were not made to limp through life. You are a living, breathing expression of God. This is Glory Days living.

Personal Actions

Now take some time to put the principles discussed during this session into practice.

"I'm with Him"

The simple cartoon with the lamb walking "hand in hand" with Jesus illustrates a powerful and life-changing truth. God *does* fight for us, and when we walk close to Jesus, we can be confident and secure just because we are with him.

When threats come and enemies of any sort are near, declare the words, "I'm with him!" Say it and mean it. You might even want to say it out loud. Write these words somewhere you will see them on a regular basis. When you see the words, declare the truth and walk in bold confidence.

Glory Days Declaration

As you wrap up your sixth and final week of *Glory Days*, don't forget the lessons you have learned. If you have not done so already, take time to memorize the brief Glory Days declaration. Let these words become a personal statement of truth and hope:

> *These days are Glory Days.*
> *My past is past,*
> *my future is bright,*
> *God's promises are true and his Word is sure.*
> *With God as my helper,*
> *I will be all he wants me to be,*
> *do all he wants me to do,*
> *and receive all he wants me to receive.*
> *These are the Glory Days.*

Here are some ways you can use this declaration in the coming weeks and months:

- Use it as you start your day for the next couple of weeks. When you wake up, before you get out of bed, say quietly, "These days are Glory Days." Then pray for God's presence and power to be unleashed as you enter into your day.
- When you break for lunch, say the Glory Days declaration when you pray for your meal, and ask yourself if you have been living a Glory Day so far. If you have wandered from an attitude of confident hope in God, make adjustments that will guide you through the rest of your day.
- When you hit a hard situation and conflict or pain are near, say the Glory Days declaration. Invite the Holy Spirit to remind you of the truth of who you are and what God calls you to be.
- As you see God show up and do great things in your life and in the world around you, use this simple declaration as a trigger to thank God for his glory and power.
- When you put your head on the pillow at the end of the day, before you doze off and fall asleep, say the Glory Days declaration. Thank God for the ways you have walked in his truth. Confess where you wandered off track and ask for grace and a fresh start.

Join in the Fight

In the session, Max told how his dad stepped in and fought for him when he was treated badly by the pastor after delivering his first sermon. Max's own father showed him the presence of his heavenly Father by stepping into the fray and protecting him.

Think about a person in your life who is being treated unfairly. If you are able to do so, step in on his or her behalf. If you feel God wants to show his presence and protecting love through you, enter in and do something.

Sometimes God fights for us by sending people who have courage to be with us in the midst of the pain and hurt of life. Young Nadin Khoury had some of the Philadelphia Eagles stand by his side. Max's dad took a stand on his behalf. Likewise, make yourself available to God and to someone who needs a helping hand.

Who do you know who needs someone to stand at his or her side?

What is that person facing? What is his or her need?

Pray, "Lord, would you have me step in, help out, and fight for _____ in your name?" If you feel God leading you to take action, what can you do?

Keep marching and believing.

Recommended Reading
As you reflect on what God is teaching you through this session, read chapter 16 of *Glory Days* by Max Lucado.

Journal, Reflections, and Notes

SMALL GROUP LEADER HELPS

To ensure a successful small group experience, read the following information before beginning.

Group Preparation

Whether your small group has been meeting together for years or is gathering for the first time, be sure to designate a consistent time and place to work through the six sessions. Once you establish the when and where of your times together, select a facilitator who will keep discussions on track and an eye on the clock. If you choose to rotate this responsibility, assign the six sessions to their respective facilitators up front so that group members can prepare their thoughts and questions prior to the session they are responsible for leading. Follow the same assignment procedure should your group want to serve any snacks/beverages.

A Note to Facilitators

As facilitator, you are responsible for honoring the agreed-upon time frame of each meeting, for prompting helpful discussion among your group, and for keeping the dialogue equitable by drawing out quieter members and helping more talkative members to remember that others' insights are valued in your group.

You might find it helpful to preview each session's video

teaching segment (they range from 23–30 minutes) and then scan the discussion questions and Bible passages that pertain to it, highlighting various questions that you want to be sure to cover during your group's meeting. Ask God in advance of your time together to guide your group's discussion, and then be sensitive to the direction he wishes to lead.

Urge participants to bring their study guide, pen, and a Bible to every gathering. Encourage them to consider buying a copy of the book *Glory Days* by Max Lucado to supplement this study.

Session Format

Each session of the study guide includes the following group components:

- **"Introduction"** — an entrée to the session's topic, which may be read by a volunteer or summarized by the facilitator
- **"Talk About It"** — icebreaker questions that relate to the session topic and invite input from every group member (select one, or use both options if time permits)
- **"Video Teaching Notes"** — an outline of the session's video teaching segment for group members to follow along and take notes if they wish
- **"Video Discussion and Bible Study"** — video-related and Bible exploration questions that reinforce the session content and elicit personal input from every group member
- **"Closing Prayer"** — several prayer cues to guide group members in closing prayer

Additionally, in each session you will find a **"Between Sessions"** section (**"In the Coming Days"** for session six) that includes a personal reflection, suggestions for personal actions, a journaling opportunity, and recommended reading from the book *Glory Days*.

NOTES

1. C. S. Lewis, *The Weight of Glory* (New York: Harper-Collins, 1949), p. 26.
2. "Fourteen False Advertising Scandals That Cost Brands Millions," *Business Insider*, http://www.businessinsider.com/false-advertising-scandals–2011–9#activia-yogurt–1.
3. This cartoon comes out of the mind of Christian comedian Ken Davis. See http://store.kendavis.com/products/I%27m-With-Him.html.

Live Your Promised Land Life Now

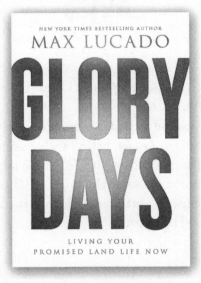

ISBN: 978-0-8499-4849-7
$26.99

You have everything you need to be everything God desires. With God's help you can close the gap between the person you are and the person you want to be.

Available wherever books and ebooks are sold.

GloryDaysBook.com

Also Available

Join us in *Jericho Unearthed* as we return to the site of one of history's most important battles in order to explore the crucial question relating to Joshua's conquest: Did the walls of Jericho really come tumbling down?